Taking Care of Our World
Revised Edition

Published by

BIoImages

P.O. Box 4537
Decatur, Illinois 62525 USA
email: BioImages@aol.com
website: www.Buffettimages.com

ISBN#0-9707385-5-2

Library of Congress Card Number: 2002092206

Printed by Tien Wah Press (Pte) Limited
4 Pandan Crescent Singapore
Color Design by Greendell Publishing

Photographs by Howard G. Buffett

Biodiversity's House

Introduction

The world's biodiversity is made up of hundreds of thousands of different ecosystems. Biodiversity is a way to refer to all the different forms of life, including plants and animals. Ecosystems are the actual areas where all these forms of life interact with each other. There are different types of ecosystems such as Forests, Wetlands, Deserts, Grasslands, Oceans, Rivers and Lakes.

Biodiversity is like nature's house. Everything in the house has a reason and a place. Some of these things are like precious gifts from your grandparents -- items that are very old and cannot be replaced. When you have something like this, you treat it carefully, you protect it, and you appreciate it. Nature is no different, it needs our protection and appreciation.

If biodiversity is nature's house, then each ecosystem is like a different room in the house. You couldn't build a house big enough to have enough rooms for each ecosystem in the world, but if you could, each room would be very special and very different. Each ecosystem has thousands of little creatures in it, and some have very large creatures.

Whether these creatures are tiny insects or large mammals, each one serves a purpose. When one creature is taken away from the ecosystem, it can create an imbalance. Think if the world had too many ants, flies or bees, or, think if there were too many elephants! It would be uncomfortable or maybe even dangerous to go outside.

But nature provides ways to keep everything in balance. Sometimes man interferes with nature's plan. When that happens, it can cause problems. By learning about different animals and their homes, we can do a better job of protecting our world.

A healthy *forest* can support many kinds of creatures. Forests provide food and shelter for many animals that depend on the forest for their home.

When a forest is destroyed to use the wood for cooking or heating or when trees are cleared to grow ***crops***, many animals lose their homes.

Many birds use trees for their houses.
This Macaw lives in a dead palm tree deep in the
jungle in *Peru*.

4

Some birds, like the Red-breasted Toucan use trees
as a source of food.

There are other birds, like this Great Egret, that are large and fly to many different forests and **wetlands** around the world.
These birds **migrate** so they can find new food during the winter.

This bird is a Kingfisher. It has a long pointed beak that helps it catch and eat small fish.

The Toco Toucan has a funny bill and he uses it to snip fruit off trees.
Toucans love all types of tropical fruit.

The Crowned Crane has an unusual crest on its head.
The crest is for decoration and helps attract a *mate*.

Other animals like this Jaguar in **Belize,** use trees for
safety and rest. The jaguar has a special coat to help **camouflage** him when he is hunting.

In **Africa**, Leopards like this one sleep in trees where it is safe. Leopards also like to hide their food in the trees; this way other animals cannot take their food away.

Pandas like to hang out in trees and play. Pandas only live in the wild in **China**. They are considered an **endangered species** because there are only about 1,000 Pandas left in the wild.

This Black Bear in *Canada* climbed this tree
to get away from another bear. Sometimes bears like this
will climb trees to get honey from a beehive.

Trees keep the soil from washing away. Without trees, waterfalls
like this one, Iguazu Falls in Brazil, would turn dirty with mud.
Without trees the **nutrients** in the soil also wash away, making it hard to grow food or plants.

Animals like the Caiman in **Brazil** spend a lot of time
in the water. When water becomes polluted, many animals
cannot survive.

A Leopard depends on fresh water both
for itself and for the animals it hunts.

Many birds depend on fresh water for fish. The Osprey's *diet* consists only of fish.
Here it swoops down to catch a fish just below the surface of the lake.
If we pollute the water, the fish die and these birds have no food.

This Brown Bear in the **United States** needs fish for **protein**.
Fish is the main diet for many bears.

This Black Bear is getting ready to sleep in its **den** for the winter. If he doesn't have enough fish from clean water and berries from healthy bushes and trees he cannot live through the winter.

Some animals, like this Fox, are **scavengers** so they eat a lot of different things, including an old sandwich from the garbage.

Other animals like this Mountain Gorilla need a lot of *vegetation* to eat.
The forests in *Uganda* where this gorilla lives are being cut down to grow crops.
If this continues, in a few years this gorilla might lose its home.

Since a good meal depends on hard work, many big cats must hunt constantly. This Lion, in *Botswana,* is a great hunter and is considered king of the jungle.

The Cheetah is the fastest land *mammal* in the world and it must hunt every few days. It hunts other animals that live in the forests and in areas called *savanna grasslands*, so the cheetah needs healthy forests and plains to survive.

There are animals like this Siberian Tiger that live in areas where it snows. Siberian tigers can be found in *Russia* and China.

In **Malaysia**, its relative, the Indochinese Tiger lives in the ***tropics*** where the weather is warm and it never snows.

In **Central and South America** this large cat is called a Puma.

But in the United States and Canada,
the same large cat is usually called a Mountain Lion or a Cougar.

Most animals make some kind of noise.
Some are calls to alert other animals about danger, some are noises that a mother
uses to call her cubs. Can you think of the noise this Zebra is making?

This Chimpanzee is making a noise because he is excited to see us! Can you guess what it sounds like?

Most animals like to play, just like you and me. Here two Tigers are wrestling.
They are **littermates**. They will stay together until they are about two or three years old and then
they will stake out their own **territory**.

These Macaws can't wrestle, so they find other ways to play and communicate.

Some animals stand out because of their color, like this Snow Monkey in *Japan*. During the winter months these monkeys spend a lot of time in *hot springs* enjoying the warm water.

Some animals blend in with their surroundings,
like this Snowy Owl in Canada. Their ability to camouflage themselves protects
them from harm by *predators*.

All young animals need their parents to take care of them.
Cheetah cubs will remain behind in a safe place when their mother hunts for food.

A curious cub is bold enough to approach a large male lion.
Lions live in **prides** and help each other take care of their young.
They also hunt together as a team.

In northern Canada, where it gets very cold, these Polar Bear cubs need their mother to keep them warm. Polar Bears have a thick coat of **fur** that *insulates* them in the winter and actually helps them stay cool in the summer!

This little Monkey stays dry and warm by hitching a ride on its mother's back.

These two young Giraffes stick close to their mother for safety.
These giraffes live in **Tanzania** in a huge ecosystem known as the **Serengeti.**

© H.W. Buffett

This Leopard cub is about seven months old. Its mother is constantly on the lookout
to protect her cub from danger, and she
needs the thick forest to hide her cub and keep her safe.

The world is a special place

with many wonderful animals.

It is our job to protect our environment

and take care of it.

If we do not save the trees and

keep the water and air clean,

then we are destroying the world we all need.

World Map

Russia

Japan

China

Malaysia

Uganda
Serengeti
Tanzania

Africa

Botswana

World Map

Canada

United States

Belize

Central America

Peru

Brazil

Glossary

Camouflage	The coloration or markings on an animal that help it blend in with its surroundings. The cheetah's spots and a tiger's stripes are its *camouflage* and help it hide from other animals.
Crops	Plants that are grown specifically for food. These include produce like corn, beans, or potatoes.
Den	The home of a wild animal. These can be a hole dug in the ground, a hollow log or a cave.
Diet	The food and drink that all living things usually eat.
Endangered Species	A plant or animal that is in danger of disappearing from the earth forever.
Forest	Thick growth of trees covering a large area of land.
Fur	The soft, thick coat covering some animals.
Hot springs	A natural flow of hot water in special places. This very hot water is heated from contact with rocks from the center of the earth.
Insulates	Providing protection from hot or cold. Some *mammals* have *fur* that *insulates* them and keeps them warm in the winter and cool in the summer.
Littermate	Two or more animals born from the same mother.
Mammal	Any warm-blooded animal whose skin is covered by hair. Female mammals produce milk to feed their young.
Mate	Either the adult male or female partner who have come together to produce offspring.
Migrate	To move from one area to another, usually with the change of the seasons.

Glossary

Nutrients A substance, like vitamins and minerals, that helps things grow and gives life to plants and animals.

Predators Animals that hunt other animals for food.

Prides A group of lions that live together like a family, usually with several adult males and females.

Protein An important part of an animal's diet.

Savanna grassland A large area of grass with very few or no trees.

Scavengers Animals that take, eat or use things that are no longer wanted or needed.

Species A distinct kind of animal or bird.

Territory An area that an animal marks as its own. Animals use these areas for hunting, breeding and living. They will defend their *territories* from use by other animals.

Tropics A region that is hot and has a lot of humidity (moisture in the air.)

Vegetation Plants that can be eaten.

Wetlands An area that is flooded with water or full of water from time to time. Most wetlands support many different types of wildlife because they produce *vegetation* which provides important *nutrients* which animals and birds need to live.

To find out what you can do to help, contact any of the following organizations:

African Wildlife Foundation
www.awf.org
e-mail: africanwildlife@awf.org

Chengdu Giant Panda Research Center
www.giantpanda.org
e-mail: pandaivf@mail.sc.cninfo.net

DeWildt Cheetah and Wildlife Trust
www.dewildt.org.za
e-mail: cheetah@dewildt.org.za

EcoTrust
www.ecotrust.org
e-mail: info@ecotrust.org

International Gorilla Conservation Program
(*A coalition of African Wildlife Foundation, World Wildlife Fund and Fauna and Flora International*)
www.awf.org
e-mail: africanwildlife@awf.org *or* Alanjouw@awfke.org

National Audubon Society
www.audubon.org
e-mail: askaudubon@audubon.org

Save the Tiger Fund
www.5tigers.org
e-mail: walmer@nfwf.org

Tiger Watch
e-mail: tigerwatch@hotmail.com

National Fish and Wildlife Foundation
www.nfwf.org
e-mail: www.nfwf.org

Wildlife Conservation Society
www.wcs.org
e-mail: pr@wcs.org

World Wildlife Fund – U.S.
www.worldwildlife.org
e-mail: membership@wwfus.org